The Word of God
FATHER   WORD   SPIRIT

Literally
THE WORD

The Word of God
FATHER WORD SPIRIT

Literally
THE WORD

by
Jerry W. Hollenbeck

Christian Literature & Artwork
A BOLD TRUTH Publication

Unless otherwise indicated all Scripture quotations are taken from the King James Version of The Bible.

The Word of God - Literally THE WORD
Copyright © 2014 Jerry Hollenbeck

ISBN 13: 978-0-9904376-5-9

BOLD TRUTH PUBLISHING
PO Box 742
Sapulpa, Oklahoma 74067
www.BoldTruthPublishing.com

I would like to dedicate this book to my wife of 24+ years. I told her 25 years ago that I felt that God would have me write a book. This is my third one. I had no idea that the Lord would give me such clear and concise revelation on His Word, and His Kingdom.

Contents

Introduction

If the trinity was ever mentioned in the Old Testament it would read, The Father, The Word, and The Spirit.

1 Jo. 5:7
For there are three that bear record in heaven, the Father, the Word, and the Holy Ghost: and these three are one.

1 Jo. 5:7 is about as close as we can get to see the imphasis we need to focus on in this book. We are not talking about Jesus, as much as we are talking about "The Word," the second person of the Godhead. Who Jesus, was before He was Jesus. He was the Word, from everlasting to everlasting, but when the Word, was made flesh...

NOW,...we have Jesus, the man, the Son of the living God!! Heb. 6:1 says,

Therefore leaving the principles of the doctrine of Christ, let us go on unto perfection,

The Word, "as always," did what God sent Him to do. He became a man on a mission to redeem mankind back to God. He came, He lived a sinless life, He took upon Himself our sin, He became sin and died on the cross in our place and gave us His righteousness, which is The Righteousness of God that the Bible talks about.

Don't forget, in this book we're not talking about Jesus, so much as we're talking about the "Word," the second person of the Godhead. When you see Him in His primary identity, old familiar scripture will take on a new dynamic, new length, breadth, and depth. You will clearly see why the words we speak can change our lives.

In Rev. 19:11-16 Jesus goes back to His original identity, THE WORD OF GOD!!

A new name for Jesus, but not a new name for who He really is, THE WORD OF GOD, will be His new name.

Psa. 138:2
I will worship toward thy holy temple, and praise thy name for thy lovingkindness and for thy truth: for thou hast magnified thy word above all thy name.

What could be more important to a man than his name? A handshake would be a good answer, but how about a man's word? If a man's word is good, the man can be depended on and counted reliable and responsible to do what he said he would do. If a mans word is no good, he cannot be depended on to do what he says.

Jer. 1:12
Then said the LORD unto me, Thou hast well seen: for I will hasten my word to perform it.

God watches over His Word and hastens to performe it. One of the problems is the fact that we don't know how to ask Him for what we want!! We have been told in several ways to renew our minds, but we havn't done it yet. At least not in any of the churches I've visited, or attended. Let's start here, change from the ways the old man thinks and does things to the ways God thinks and does things.

Col. 3:9-10
9. Lie not one to another, seeing that ye have put off the old man with his deeds;
10. And have put on the new man, which is renewed in knowledge after the image of him that created him:

There's no money in the Kingdom of God. No tools, supplies, or equipment. All we have as a rate of exchange in the Kingdom of God are the words we speak. God does everything with or by "words!!" We are going to have to learn to do the same thing, the same way!!

It's words only,...in the Kingdom of God. Words are all we have to work with in the Kingdom of God.

Right now, as a born-again believer, we can think and speak of salvation fluently, but as a child of the Kingdom, we're as dumb as a rock. We can't even think right,...how can we even attempt to speak right?

Let me give you an example that will open up a whole new realm of possibilities for you.

How does God create something from nothing? It's simple when you see it, but until you see it, it boggles the mind, there's no answer. Jesus often used natural examples to bring out a spiritual truth. So, here we go, **necessity is the mother of invention.** We'll use the sun in our own solar system as our example. God knew that we would need light on the earth so He said, LET THERE BE LIGHT!!

Contained in the word LIGHT, was all the information needed to produce the sun in our solar system. Now listen carefully, the Word, that is in Him, that is to say, the second person of the Godhead, immediately knew what God was thinking and what God intended when God said the word LIGHT, The Word 'now called Jesus' went on out in the universe and created the sun. the word LIGHT, had all the generic information in it, as a seed, to produce the sun with all its attributes.

Heb. 4:12
For the **word** *of God is* **quick, and powerful,** *and sharper than any two edged sword, piercing even to the dividing asunder of soul and spirit, and of the joints and marrow,* **and is a discerner of the thoughts and intents of the heart.**

Thoughts and intents form the blueprint and compose all the generic information in our words, Faith gives the information substance, then of course, we have the evidence of things not seen at the time we prayed, transformed into this natural realm.

Hey Bubba, the Word of God, the second person of the Godhead, now lives in you the same way He was in God when God said, LET THERE BE LIGHT!! And the Word went out and created the sun.

What are you saying about your situations,

conditions, tests and trials that seem to come in on every wave?

Are you saying what your experience in the world has taught you? We just can't make it. Just as sure as we get there, they'll be sold out. Nothing ever works out for me anyway. No paycheck is ever enough. OR, are you saying what your Father is trying to teach you? I can do all things through Christ that strengthens me. Nothing shall be impossible to me. All things work for good for me. I am in need of no aid or assistance from anybody for anything, I have all sufficiency for all things thoroughly furnished to all good works. Nothing by any means shall hurt me.

We are all living "right now" in the sum of our words. Like it or not, know it or not, accept it or not, believe it or not doesn't even matter. The truth is we are living in the sum of our words up until now!! If you don't like the way life is treating you, CHANGE-YOUR-WORDS!! IT'S WORDS ONLY, IN THE KINGDOM OF GOD!!

No money, no silver, no gold or precious stones. God lives by His Words, and He's teaching us to do the same thing, the same way, and get the desired results. So,...when you see a need, speak it, frame it with words just like

God did in Genesis, doubt not in your heart, but believe what you said shall come to pass, and Jesus said, you will have what you said.

Jo. 14:13-14
13. And whatsoever ye shall ask in my name, that will I do, that the Father may be glorified in the Son.
14. If ye shall ask any thing in my name, I will do it.

Jesus does everything God says. Jesus just told you that He will do everything that you say in His name.

If you leave your prayer, EXPECTING, that's faith!! And Jesus will confirm the Word, with signs following.

If you're not EXPECTING, you're not in Faith and Jesus is not obligated to confirm your request with signs following. RIGHT?

Am I saying "all" the words that we speak? Whether they be spoken in anger or haste, or words spoken in jest or speculation, by assumption or even a curse spoken against someone? No, no, certainly not!! Only those words that we doubt not in our hearts, but believe will come to pass. Isn't that what

Jesus said in Mk. 11:23? *Whatsoever a man says, doubts not in his heart, but shall believe that those things which he says shall come to pass; he shall have whatsoever he said.*

Chapter 1
Sowing The Word

Over the past five years I have found it amazing of how many preachers, pastors, and teachers simply are not interested in hearing about the Kingdom of God. However, in my meetings the people can't get enough. They love the teachings that the Lord has shared with me concerning the Kingdom of God. It's not the first thing Jesus said do, but it is the one thing that Jesus said, do this first! What was He talking about when He said that? What are we going to eat, what are we going to drink, and wherewithal shall we be clothed? In other words,

"the issues of life."

Mt. 6:33
But seek ye first the kingdom of God, and his righteousness; and all these things shall be added unto you.

We are getting a lot of teaching about

building walls of protection, unforgiveness, judgementalism, the Blood, the Cross, the Resurrection, Godly behavior, and such but where's the gospel of the Kingdom? Don't get me wrong, we need to know about all these things, but we also need to know how to live the overcoming life that God has prepared for those who love Him. Besides that, none of those issues will pay the rent next month. How are we to buy a home today, or get a safe dependable car, or send our children to college?

Well hey brother, you're going to have to have a really good job and make a lot of money to do those things. Every month,... a lot of money!! But what if you don't have a good job? In case you haven't noticed, you're not going to do well in this natural world without a steady income and a lot of money.

If someone were to ask you, you could probably answer this question correctly, but I still think you will be shocked when I tell you, there's no money in the Kingdom of God. Not one dime. No monetary value at all. No money, no silver, no gold, nothing that a man can reach into his pocket to give, or trade for goods or services. What we have is better than choice silver, and more costly than fine gold. It is outrageous in it's buying power and dynamic in it's working. We have a heavenly or supernatural rate of exchange. Jesus called it The True Riches, but He didn't explain what the true riches are.

Isa. 55:1

Ho, every one that thirsteth, come ye to the waters, and he that hath no money; come ye, buy, and eat; yea, come, buy wine and milk <u>without money and without price.</u>

We all could have our gardens full of the true riches, but since we don't recognize them as riches we would be inclined to weed them out and throw them away. We live in an agrarian society. We're Bible thumping farmers. We sow the Word of God, and reap the harvest (or fruit of the) blessing. Notice I said "the" blessing, not "a" blessing.

Each promise of God is designed to produce "the" specific fruit it describes. Oh yes, the promises are given,... to produce the answers to our needs. What are we going to eat, drink, and wherewithal shall we be clothed?

Mk. 4:14-15
14. The sower soweth the word.

15. And these are they by the way side, where the word is sown; but when they have heard,

Satan cometh immediately, and taketh away **the word that was sown in their hearts.**

We sow the Word of God into the heart of the person we're ministering to, or "our own heart" and that seed of the Word of God will produce whatsoever it described. In time of need, find a promise that covers your need, speak it, doubt not in your heart, but believe what you prayed shall come to pass!!

Mk. 4:21-29

21. And he said unto them, Is a candle brought to be put under a bushel, or under a bed? and not to be set on a candlestick?

22. For there is nothing hid, which shall not be manifested; neither was any thing kept secret, but that it should come abroad.

23. If any man have ears to hear, let him hear.

24. And he said unto them, Take heed what ye hear: with what measure ye mete, it shall be measured to you: and unto you that hear shall more be given.

25. For he that hath, to him shall be given: and he that hath not, from him shall be taken even that which he hath.

26. And he said, So is the kingdom of God, as if a man should cast seed into the ground;

27. And should sleep, and rise night and

*day, and the seed should **spring and grow up**, he knoweth not how.*

28. ***For the earth bringeth forth fruit of herself;*** *first the blade, then the ear, after that the full corn in the ear.*

29. *But when the fruit is brought forth, immediately he putteth in the sickle, because the harvest is come.*

Come on Church, have you got it yet? Words,...Words are the true riches!! Words are the accepted legal tender in the Kingdom of God. The "only" rate of exchange in the Kingdom of God!! Not just any words, words that are accompanied with thought, intent, and **expectation**!!!

Heb. 4:12
For the word of God is quick, and powerful, *and sharper than any twoedged sword, piercing even to the dividing asunder of soul and spirit, and of the joints and marrow,* ***and is a discerner of the thoughts and intents of the heart.***

In the form of the promises, "seeds" God has given us what to say. By releasing Faith when we speak or proclaim a thing, that's what puts our words in motion. When we walk away from our prayer, **"expecting!!"** that's Faith.

If we walk away from our prayer not expecting, Jesus, is not obligated to confirm our words with signs following. Our words did not return to God filled with Faith. They immediately fell to the ground to be trodden under foot ineffective, dysfunctional, and idle words.

Mt. 12:36-37

*36. But I say unto you, That **every idle word that men shall speak**, they shall give account thereof in **the day of judgment.***

37. For by thy words thou shalt be justified, and by thy words thou shalt be condemned.

When is the day of judgment? The day you spoke and your words fell to the ground, and did not return to God filled with Faith. Don't be stupid. The Word is in you. He knows whether you're believing for the petition or not. We need to speak words accompanied with thought, intent, AND EXPECTATION!!

When you received Jesus as savior, you received the Word of God in your heart. He is in you exactly the same way He was in God when God said, Let there be Light!! And the Word, went out and created light. Then by the grace of God, the Word came along in John 14:13-14. And said, whatever you say, I'll do it!!

Come on Church, think! It was the Word, on salvation that produced salvation. It'll be the Word, on healing that will produce healing. The Word, is a person, we only now call Him Jesus, but before He was Jesus, He was "The Word of God."

If so be that ye have heard him, and have been taught by him, as the truth is in Jesus:
Ephesians 4:21

Chapter 2
The Word of God

_Jo. 1:1-4_
1. In the beginning was the Word, and the Word was with God, and the Word was God.

2. *The same was in the beginning with God.*

3. All things were made by him; and without him was not any thing made that was made.

4. *In him was life; and the life was the light of men.*

Eph. 5:14-17

14. *Wherefore he saith, Awake thou that sleepest, and arise from the dead, and Christ shall give thee light.*

15. *See then that ye walk circumspectly, not as fools, but as wise,*

16. *Redeeming the time, because the days are evil.*

17. *Wherefore be ye not unwise,* **_but understanding what the will of the Lord is._**

THE PROMISES ARE GOD'S WILL FOR HIS PEOPLE!!

__1 Jo. 5:14-15__
*14. And this is the **confidence** that we have in him, that, if we ask any thing according to his **will,** he heareth us:*
*15. And if we know that he hear us, **whatsoever we ask**, we know that we **have the petitions** that we desired of him.*

In my most recent Bible training school which was a nine month course. Out of a student body of 45 students we were split up into small groups of 4 to 6 people. Our assignment was to pioneer a church somewhere. After we picked a city, we had to figure our budget. What it would cost to move there, lodging costs, facility, gas, electric, phone, advertising and etc. We determined who was going to be the Pastor, the praise and worship leader, the administrator/bookkeeper, and my job was to be the Sunday school teacher. I chose as my main subject, The Kingdom of God, and His Righteousness. Otherwise known as the "Kingdom Realities" research and development classes.

Little did I know that God was going to send me on a far, far journey where not many men have gone before.

When I speak of "not many men" I'm speaking of the body of Christ, and not many men in the body have done this. You can tell by what they preach. Is it Kingdom truth, or is it Christianity the religion, don't do this and don't do that?

Do you remember the TV show The Cosmos? From a small TV stage set designed much like the bridge of the starship Enterprise, an astrologer took us throughout the universe showing us galaxies, nebulas, black holes, quasars and such. He showed us how planets were formed, lived, and died.

Where we are going in this little book, may as well be light years away from here. It cannot be seen by the naked eye, but anyone and everyone can see the evidence of it. Jesus said, the Kingdom is within us. The devil has blinded our minds to it before we were saved, and now, the only way we will ever see or experience it ourselves is to renew our minds to it. And that's something that the overwhelming majority of the body of Christ has not done yet.

When you got saved, God, didn't renew your mind from the things of the world to the things of God, or His Kingdom.

WOW, God, really missed it there didn't He?

OH, WAIT!! He told **us** to do that!!!

Ro. 12:2

And be not conformed to this world: but be ye transformed by the renewing of your mind, that ye may prove what is that good, and acceptable, and perfect, will of God.

Eph. 4:20-24

20. But ye have not so learned Christ;

21. If so be that ye have heard him, and have been taught by him, as the truth is in Jesus:

22. That ye put off concerning the former conversation the old man, which is corrupt according to the deceitful lusts;

23. And be renewed in the spirit of your mind;

24. And that ye put on the new man, which after God is created in righteousness and true holiness.

Col. 3:9-10

9. Lie not one to another, seeing that ye have put off the old man with his deeds;

*10. And have put on the new man, which is **renewed in knowledge** after the image of him that created him:*

Out of the mouth of two or three witnesses, let every word be established.

This is where Christianity "the religion" has missed it all these years. We thought God, was going to renew our minds, and we're still waiting!! Son, daughter, God has already done all He intends to do. As a matter of fact, the Bible says the "works" were finished from the foundation of the world.

Heb. 4:3
For we which have believed do enter into rest, as he said, As I have sworn in my wrath, if they shall enter into my rest: although the works were finished from the foundation of the world.

*So mightily grew the word of God
and prevailed.
Acts 19:20*

Chapter 3
A Wealth of Words

So, how are we to live this life that God has prepared for those who love Him? 1 Co. 2:9. In a word,...Words. Faith filled words. The truth be known, we received all the wealth we will ever need the moment we were born again. The thing is, we don't recognize our wealth, so we can't possibly spend it or make our way through life by using it.

Do you remember how Jesus, talked about money? He didn't like money. He called it unrighteous mammon, filthy lucre. Then He mentioned the true riches but did not describe what the true riches are.

Lu. 16:11
If therefore ye have not been faithful in the unrighteous mammon, who will commit to your trust the true riches?

We cannot calculate our true wealth because it comes in such abundance. How can you measure the intrinsic value of,... Words? No matter what goes on out there in the world, we have plenty to say about it. We'll never run out of words. However, we have a choice, are we going to say what the world has taught us, or are we going to say what God is teaching us? We can speak the cursing that the world has taught us, or we can speak the blessings that God is teaching us. (All the promises in God are not yea and nay, but in Him is yea and amen!!!)

Remember what God said, in,...

Deut. 30:19
I call heaven and earth to record this day against you, that I have set before you life and death, blessing and cursing: therefore choose life, that both thou and thy seed may live:

Our heavenly Father has given us a free will. The thing is, God's words are able to overcome what the world says and bring it to not. Everything in the world and on the planet is subject to change,....the Word of God, is not subject to change, neither is there a shadow of turning with God.

I write a lot of stuff about the Kingdom of God. It used to be that I would compare everything that goes on out there to the Bible. Today however, I compare everything to the "knowledge" of the Kingdom. Casting down every imagination, and high thing that exalts itself against the "knowledge" of God, bringing into captivity every thought to the obedience of Christ. ("The Word")

There are laws that govern the Kingdom of God. There are laws that govern the power of God. If we can get in line with these laws, we can live an overcoming life of the demonstration of the Spirit, and of power. These laws are given in the form of promises, truths, and Spiritual laws. The thing is, the Kingdom laws and the power laws are the same laws, ...THE PROMISES!!!

We have the blessing of dealing with exact knowledge, knowledge that is so exact, so accurate and focused, it qualifies to be a truth. That's not all though. God's knowledge is so exact, so accurate, so true that it qualifies to be a law. God said it, put it in motion for us to use thousands of years ago and it "the knowledge" will still produce or manifest itself today. The power to produce is actually in the Words themselves, ...as seeds.

Jo. 1:1-3
1. In the beginning was the Word, and the

Word was with God, and the Word was God.

2. The same was in the beginning with God.

3. All things were made by him; and without him was not any thing made that was made.

God is restoring knowledge to the body of Christ, in these last days of harvest so that outsiders can see that Christians are walking the walk, and talking the talk, and changing things within their realm of influence on the earth.

I'm thinking that if we knew how the Word works, we would be more embolden to use the Word more in our life circumstances, tests, and trials. I hope you enjoy this little journey into the "knowledge" of the Kingdom

We need to learn to live according to our words like our Father God does. Jesus said, Jo.6:63. It is the spirit that quickeneth; the flesh profiteth nothing: the words that I speak unto you, they are spirit, and they are life.

Until we renew our minds from the way the world thinks and does things, to the way God thinks and does things, our words are still mans wisdom, not Spirit and life.

Can we do this? Can we make this change from carnal knowledge to Spiritual knowledge?

This change is only for those who have ears to hear it!! Do all speak in tongues, do all prophesy? No, No. Can every person make this change? YES!!

Will every person make this change? Sadly no, only those who have ears to hear and purpose in their heart to renew their minds to God's thoughts and ways will be able to do this.

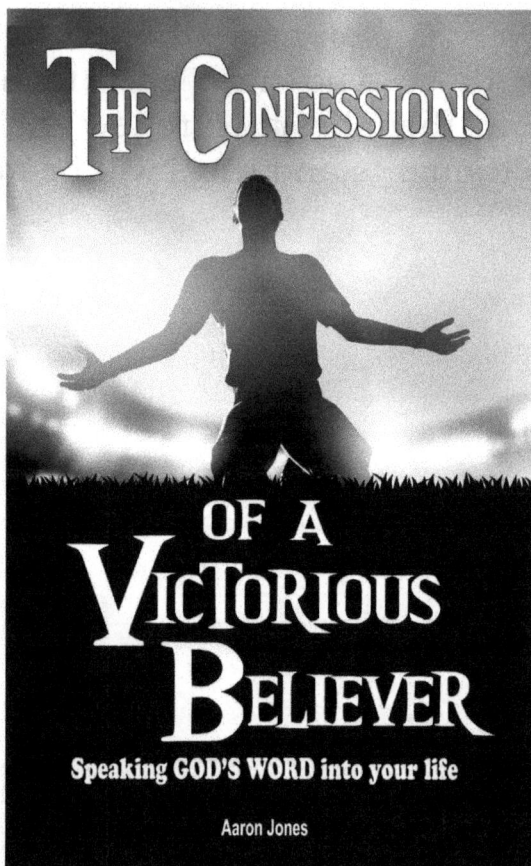

Chapter 4
Jesus is The Word

We're going to be talking about the Word of God. Not the Bible as such, and not of Jesus the man. We're talking about the Word now, in the beginning when it had no name or designated gender. "It" was the Word of God.

Jo. 1:1-3
1. In the beginning was the Word, and the Word was with God, and the Word was God.

2. The same was in the beginning with God.

3. All things were made by him; and without him was not any thing made that was made.

In **Jo. 1:"1&2"** we see the old testament picture of the Word of God. In **Jo. 1:3** we now see the Word, being called him. That's the new testament picture of the man Jesus Christ, the Son of God. Jesus had a beginning just like you and I, the Word did not! The Word, always was and always will be. Our focus in this study is the Old Testament Word of God, not the New Testament man Jesus of Nazareth. I know it's difficult to make the distinction between the Word and Jesus the man, but in order to understand this study, you must do it.

Jesus is the Word of God, and it is Jesus, The Word, that is going to perform the doing of what we ask for in prayer.

Jo. 14:13-14
13. And whatsoever ye shall ask in my name, that will I do, that the Father may be glorified in the Son.
*14. If ye shall ask any thing in my name, **I will do it.***

In Prov. 7:4 Jesus "The Word", is called wisdom, our sister and understanding our kinswoman. In other places He, was called "the angel of the Lord." however,..in the Old Testament, God called Him "IT".

1 Co. 1:23-24
23. But we preach Christ crucified, unto the Jews a stumblingblock, and unto the Greeks foolishness;
*24. But unto them which are called, both Jews and Greeks, **Christ the power of God, and the wisdom of God.***

Here is a good example of how I'm trying

to show you the difference between The Word, and Jesus, the man.

God said, Light Be!! And the "Word" performed the doing of what God had said, and went out in space and created the sun. God has placed His creative power in His "Word"!! As pertaining to salvation, God said, Gen. 3:15 **And I will put enmity between thee and the woman, and between thy seed and her seed; it shall bruise thy head, and thou shalt bruise his heel.** Since a spirit can't be nailed to a tree, the "Word" became flesh, and now, we have the man Jesus, The Word, made flesh. The Word, in the form of a man, performed the doing of what God said. The Word came and took upon Himself our sin, died on the tree, and was resurrected again, and we are born-again "in Him." New creatures. Ones that had never existed before. He being the first born from the dead, and we in Him. What a wonderful truth!!

So shall my word be that goeth forth out of my mouth: it shall not return unto me void, but it shall accomplish that which I please, and it shall prosper in the thing whereto I sent it.
Isaiah 55:11

Chapter 5
The Word's Power

Heb. 6:1-8

1. Therefore leaving the principles of the doctrine of Christ, let us go on unto perfection; not laying again the foundation of repentance from dead works, and of faith toward God,

2. Of the doctrine of baptisms, and of laying on of hands, and of resurrection of the dead, and of eternal judgment.

3. **And this will we do, if God permit.**

4. For it is impossible for those who were <u>once enlightened, and have tasted of the heavenly gift,</u> and were made partakers of the Holy Ghost,

5. <u>And have tasted the good word of God, and the powers of the world to come,</u>

6. If they shall fall away, to renew them again unto repentance; seeing they crucify to themselves the Son of God afresh, and put him to an open shame.

7. <u>For the earth which drinketh in the rain that cometh oft upon it, and bringeth forth herbs meet for them by whom it is dressed, receiveth</u>

blessing from God:

8. But that which beareth thorns and briers is rejected, and is nigh unto cursing; whose end is to be burned.

Note: *verse 7 For the earth which drinketh in the rain that cometh oft upon it, and bringeth forth herbs meet for them by whom it is dressed, receiveth blessing from God:*

Now compare this to...

Isa. 55:10-11

10. For as the rain cometh down, and the snow from heaven, and returneth not thither, but watereth the earth, and maketh it bring forth and bud, that it may give seed to the sower, and bread to the eater:

11. So shall my word be that goeth forth out of my mouth: it shall not return unto me void, but it shall accomplish that which I please, and it shall prosper in the thing whereto I sent it.

Rain waters the earth that it brings forth and buds, so we have grass , trees, bushes, wheat, barley, and such. Right? The water doesn't go back to the atmosphere until it does it's job. It waters the earth. God is saying that His Word will be like that. It will come down, water the earth (the hearts of men), that it brings forth and buds, *Mk. 4:28 For the earth bringeth forth fruit of herself; first the blade, then the ear, after that the full corn in the ear.]* God's Word will not return to Him void, empty, ineffective or dysfunctional. It "The Word" will accomplish that which God pleases, and it "The Word" will prosper in the thing whereto God has sent it. My point is this. The same Word God released in Genesis, now lives in us who believe. The Word came up one day, in the form of the man Christ Jesus and said,

Jo. 14:13-14
13. And whatsoever ye shall ask in my name, that will I do, that the Father may be glorified in the Son.
14. If ye shall ask any thing in my name, I will do it.]

Now, in New Testament truth, the Word is saying that "I do,... whatever God says"!! And now, the Word is saying,.... I will do whatever YOU say,.... "in My name.

The sower sows the word. The word sown, is The Word of God. According to Mk. 4:15, the word is sown into the hearts of men and it grows,....

<u>Mk. 4:28</u>

For the earth bringeth forth fruit of herself; first the blade, then the ear, after that the full corn in the ear.

HOW DOES IT WORK?

<u>Gen. 1:3, 6, 9, 11, 14, 24, & 26.</u> God said, and it was so. God said, and it was so. God said, and it was so. Over and over again. And God saw that it was good, or very good.

As we see here God, doesn't have any natural tools. He merely speaks, and what He says happens or takes place. We can also use the Biblical way of saying it, God speaks, and what He says comes to pass.

OK, what we're going to see here is the fact that the Word, was in God, and that the "Word," is God's tool by which He does things.

For you computer geeks, think of your computer as God's Word to us, The Bible. Then think of the keyboard as our prayer system. Jesus, is our Word Processor. Our prayer requests are now displayed on the screen. Let's use "Let there be Light" as our example.

When God said let there be light, the Word

that was in Him knew what God was thinking, and what God intended,...immediately!! Even as God was speaking, the Word that was in Him knew what God intended. The Word immediately shot out into the universe and created the sun.

Jo. 1:3
All things were made by him; and without him was not any thing made that was made.

But that's not all. The Word knew that the sun would not have a solid surface and would give off light rays, gamma rays, ultra violet rays. There would be solar storms, nuclear fission going on and millions of degrees of heat. Now that's only a few attributes of the sun. my point is, the "Word" knew what God was thinking and what God intended. ...and God saw that it was good. In other words, it was done right.

Gen. 1:3-4
3. And God said, Let there be light: and there was light.

4. And God saw the light, that it was good: and God divided the light from the darkness.

When God said that, the "Word" went out and did it. I don't know the exact Bible translation, but for this study let's read these verses like this.

Gen. 1:3-4

3. And God said, Let there be light: and there was light. **(The Word created the light)**

4. And God saw the light, that it was good: and **_"The Word"_** *divided the light from the darkness.*

Why did I say it that way? Because the "Word" was in God, and the "Word" was God, all things were made by him; and without him was not any thing made that was made.

When God says something, the "Word" manifests what God said.!! God for some reason has put the power to produce what He says,..."in the words themselves." he likens His Word to a seed. Every seed produces after it's own kind. What's my point? By whose strips we were healed is designed to produce healing!! No weapon formed against me shall prosper, is designed to produce, no weapon formed against you shall prosper. What do you think, no plague shall come nigh thy dwelling, will produce? It was the "Word" on salvation that produced salvation. It's the "Word" on prosperity, that will produce prosperity. In case you didn't notice, God is not going to prosper you. He sent His "Word" to prosper you just as He sent His "Word" to heal you. Let God's words not depart from your thinking and from your mouth, and you will have good success in life. Else, how shall you escape, if you neglect so great salvation?

Isa. 55:8-11

8. For my thoughts are not your thoughts, neither are your ways my ways, saith the LORD.

9. For as the heavens are higher than the earth, so are my ways higher than your ways, and my thoughts than your thoughts.

10. For as the rain cometh down, and the snow from heaven, and returneth not thither, but watereth the earth, and maketh it bring forth and bud, that it may give seed to the sower, and bread to the eater:

11. So shall my word be that goeth forth out of my mouth: it shall not return unto me void, but it shall accomplish that which I please, and it shall prosper in the thing whereto I sent it.

God doesn't have a chainsaw or a cordless drill or a half inch wrench. He uses Words to produce what He wants.

Let's go through Isa. 55:8-11. Verse by verse.

8. For my thoughts are not your thoughts, neither are your ways my ways, saith the LORD.

If God wanted to build a house for you as a gift today He would not go out and buy lumber and nails, concrete and sheetrock, no, no, He would merely speak it and the "Word" of God would produce it. His thoughts are higher than our thoughts, and His ways are higher than our ways.

If you wanted to build a house for God, well now we'll have to go out and get some wood, nails, concrete, and sheetrock. Why? Because we don't think the same way God thinks and we don't do things the same way God does things. Enough said?

9. For as the heavens are higher than the earth, so are my ways higher than your ways, and my thoughts than your thoughts.

God thinks differently than we do. He sees the end from the beginning, the whole picture. That's why we need to renew our minds from the way we think, and do things, to the way God thinks, and does things. Through the promises, like God, we can see the end from the beginning of our circumstances. God is teaching us to find a promise that covers our need, speak it, doubt not, but believe we receive it even as we are praying the request. Jesus said, for anyone that would do that, they shall have what they said!! RIGHT?

10. For as the rain cometh down, and the snow from heaven, and returneth not thither, but watereth the earth, and maketh it bring forth and bud, that it may give seed to the sower, and bread to the eater:

Rain comes down and waters the earth that it bring forth and bud thereby giving a fruitful harvest. Things grow, plants produce.

11. So shall my word be that goeth forth out of my mouth: it shall not return unto me void, but it shall accomplish that which I please, and it shall prosper in the thing whereto I sent it.

God is saying that His Word will do the same thing. As a mater of fact, God's Word is specifically designed to do exactly that!! God's Word is designed to produce what it says, or describes, to the letter, to the size, to the quantity, color, exactly precisely, what God was thinking, and what God intended!!

Can we do the same thing? YES!! After.... we renew our minds to the way God thinks and does things. However, you might consider this fact, Spiritual Laws are in effect all the time. Otherwise Genesis 11:5-9 would not have had to be written. Guard your words, Mk.11:23 will work for you, or against you. By YOUR OWN words, you can overcome, or be defeated. Out of the abundance of the heart, the mouth speaketh. Life and death are in the power of the tongue. For by thy words thou shalt be justified, and by thy words thou shalt be condemned. IT'S WORDS ONLY,...IN THE KNIGDOM OF GOD!!!!!

How can we think and do things like God in the here and now? By the Righteousness of God, freely given to us when we were born-again, we can exercise that righteousness as a way of life...in the Kingdom of God,...in the here and now, not having to wait for the great by-n-by. Kingdom rule...on the earth... beginning as soon as we learn how to control our words, and think like God thinks, and do things like God does things. Looking unto Jesus the author and finisher of our faith,

Ro.12:2
And be not conformed to this world: but be ye transformed by the renewing of your mind, that ye may prove what is that good, and acceptable, and perfect, will of God.

God is not going to prove anything, WE ARE TO PROVE, what is that good, and acceptable, and perfect will of God.

Don't be stupid, don't be naïve, if you knew you were in charge of your life, things would be different!!! Wouldn't they? You bet they would!! The fact is, you are in charge, you are in control of your life. It all depends on your words, and how you intend for them to produce.

But what saith it? The word is nigh thee, even in thy mouth, and in thy heart: that is, the word of faith, which we preach;
Romans 10:8

Chapter 6
Our Words

_Ro. 12:2_
And be not conformed to this world: but be ye transformed by the renewing of your mind, that ye may prove what is that good, and acceptable, and perfect, will of God.

Did you notice that God is not going to prove anything? We,... are supposed to prove what is that good, acceptable, and perfect will of God!!! Can we actually learn how to think the way God thinks and do things the way God does things?...........**Yes!** Through the promises of God, recorded in the Bible, like God, we can see the end from the beginning of our circumstances. God calls things that be not as though they were. When we feel symptoms, we can go to the "Word," find a promise that covers our need, speak it, doubt not in our hearts, but believe what we said shall come to pass. Jesus said, if any man would do that, he would have what he said!!

Mk. 4:23-29

23. If any man have ears to hear, let him hear.

24. And he said unto them, Take heed what ye hear: with what measure ye mete, it shall be measured to you: and unto you that hear shall more be given.

25. For he that hath, to him shall be given: and he that hath not, from him shall be taken even that which he hath.

26. And he said, So is the kingdom of God, as if a man should cast seed into the ground;

27. And should sleep, and rise night and day, and the seed should spring and grow up, he knoweth not how.

28. For the earth bringeth forth fruit of herself; first the blade, then the ear, after that the full corn in the ear.

29. But when the fruit is brought forth, immediately he putteth in the sickle, because the harvest is come.

The promises of God are seeds for this life in the flesh. They are designed to produce what they describe. They will get us into what we want into and out of what we want out of. Why would a man ask God to help with the down payment for a house when he could just as easily ask God for the house,...period!! No down payment, with no monthly mortgage payments at all. Let's see it in action.

Verse 10
For as the rain cometh down, and the snow from heaven, and returneth not thither, but watereth the earth, and maketh it bring forth and bud, that it may give seed to the sower, and bread to the eater:

Water and snow, water the earth and things grow. Have you ever seen a desert picture taken just after a rain? Of course you have. The desert blossoms with flowers and grass. It's beautiful. Note that the rain does not return to the atmosphere without doing its job, the earth brings forth and buds, providing seed for the sower, And bread for the eater.

Let me give you the testimony of what happened when God revealed Mk. 11:23. to me one night in Dec. 1985. I was home alone, watching TV one night when out of the blue God dropped Mk. 11:23. Straight down into my heart.

Mk. 11:23
For verily I say unto you, That whosoever shall say unto this mountain, Be thou removed, and be thou cast into the sea; and shall not doubt in his heart, but shall believe that those

things which he saith shall come to pass; he shall have whatsoever he saith.

Well, after my eyes got as big as silver dollars and I sucked all the air out of the room and calmed down, I did a very carnal thing. I asked God for a new Jeep Cherokee. At the time I was driving a 1970 Ford van. After asking God for a new Jeep, I went to the front door of the house and declared to the front yard, I have a new Jeep!!!!!

I asked my Heavenly Father for it and like a certain preacher I know of, I'm declaring in Jesus, name,…I'm pregnant with a new Jeep, it's mine, I've asked Dad for it,… and Dad said yes!!!

Well,… a few days into this "confession of faith" I realized that this was going to take a lot of money because I asked for it to come paid for. Every once in a while I would go to the front door and declare to the front yard, IT"S COMING!! I'VE ASKED FOR IT,…. I RECEIVED IT WHEN I PRAYED,…. AND IT'S COMING!! "AND ALL MY BILLS ARE PAID." My bills being paid just kind of slipped out of my mouth. Also, my new Jeep was transforming into a new truck, not a Jeep anymore. THE "Word" is in me. He knows my thoughts and

<u>my intents **and the desires of my heart.**</u>

Knowing that this was going to take a lot of money, I started sowing money into TV ministries and helped my ex-wife with some bills. Meanwhile, my mother, who knew nothing about what I was believing for, came into an inheritance from a great Aunt. I don't know what the amount of the inheritance was, and I don't know why Mom decided to share it with me, but I do know what mom gave me, $22,000.00.

It was almost three months to the day that I asked the Lord for the new Jeep. Now during the faith-time between the initial asking and the actual manifestation, I saw a Dodge Ram Charger. Understand I was still confessing and believing for a new vehicle, but my desire had changed and now my faith was for the Dodge 4x4.

I still have the picture from the dealership when I and my son picked up the truck. It was a beautiful '86 Dodge Ram Charger, Black, four-wheel drive, mag spoke wheels, with a Red interior. Beautiful,... just Beautiful!! And I paid off all my bills.

At the end of the day, I had a friend who had a kidney transplant and was getting behind on some of his bills so I gave him what was left over from the twenty two thousand, which was right at $450.00.

A few months went by, but one day it was as though the Lord came up behind me, put His hand on my shoulder and said, "You see there son, I give seed for the sower, and bread for the eater. You got your truck, and you sowed into the life of a friend.

Verse 11
So shall my word be that goeth forth out of my mouth: it shall not return unto me void, but it shall accomplish that which I please, and it shall prosper in the thing whereto I sent it.

So shall my word be that goeth forth out of my mouth.   Like rain and/or snow.

...it shall not return unto me void, It will not return to God w/o faith, ...empty, fruitless, or dysfunctional.

but it shall accomplish that which I please, the promises are God's will for His people.

and it shall prosper in the thing whereto I sent it. The "Word of God" is designed to produce what It says or describes.

Chapter 7
The Right Words

Just as when you were born of Mom & Dad, you had to learn how to talk and live life in this natural world. Now that you have received Jesus as savior, you have been born of God. You need to learn how to talk and live in the Kingdom of God. Jesus said, my words, they are spirit and they are life. Your words need to become spirit, and life.

Let's observe how the world talks; I can't do this, this is impossible, this will never work, oh, this is to die for.

Now how does God want us to speak in His Kingdom? I can do all things through Christ, ("The Word") who strengthens me. Nothing, shall by any means hurt me. I overcome by the Blood of the Lamb and the word of my testimony. Nothing shall be impossible unto me. Himself took my infirmities and bare my sicknesses, and by His strips, I was healed. **Col. 1:13,** says we have been delivered from the power of darkness and translated into the Kingdom of God. We need to learn to live life here, in the Kingdom. Words are not my natural forte. OK, OK, I'll admit it, Spiritual words are not my forte either, but I'm learning. We all need to (as babes in Christ) learn how to talk the way our Father talks and think the way our father thinks.

The closest man has come to the God kind of Faith is, the power of positive thinking. Though they write books about it, they don't know what it is, or how it works. It's quite simple, whatever a man is thinking about sooner or later, **comes out his mouth!!**

<u>Mk. 11:23</u>
For verily I say unto you, That whosoever shall say unto this mountain, Be thou removed, and be thou cast into the sea; and shall not doubt in his heart, but shall believe that those things which he saith shall come to pass; he shall have whatsoever he saith.

<u>**Mk. 11:23**</u> is given for a blessing but can it be perverted? **Yes!!** By saying what the world has taught us to say, we can speak curses on people, ourselves, and even our loved ones.

• Oh sweetheart, I know the flu season is here and you get it every year and there's nothing we can do about it.

• By the time we get there, there won't be any left.

• If you don't straighten up, you'll be in prison by the time you're eighteen.

• Why bother, it won't work anyway.

The "Word" works whenever we put it to work. How do we put it to work? We speak a thing, doubt not in our heart, but believe what we said shall come to pass. Simple, but be careful!!

So, there is something about that "name it and clam" it, "blab it and grab it" doctrine after all. Oh yeah, the "Word works. Not just any words, just the words that are accompanied with thought, intent, belief, expectation, or the God kind of faith.

Prov. 18:21
Death and life *are* **in the power of the tongue**: and they that love it shall eat the fruit thereof.

Prov. 6:2

Thou art **snared** with **the words of thy mouth**, thou art **taken** with the **words of thy mouth**.

Prov. 4:20-24

20. My son, attend to my words; incline thine ear unto my sayings.

21. Let them not depart from thine eyes; <u>keep them in the midst of thine heart</u>.

22. <u>For they *are* **life** unto those that find them, **and health to all their flesh.**</u>

23. <u>Keep thy **heart** with all diligence; **for out of it *are* the issues of life.**</u>

24. **<u>Put away from thee a froward mouth, and perverse lips put far from thee.</u>**

Mt. 12:33-37

*33. Either make the tree good, and his fruit good; or else make the tree corrupt, and his fruit corrupt: **<u>for the tree is known by his fruit.</u>***

*34. O generation of vipers, how can ye, being evil, speak good things? **<u>for out of the abundance of the heart the mouth speaketh.</u>***

35. A good man out of the good treasure of the heart bringeth forth good things: and an evil man out of the evil treasure bringeth forth evil things.

36. But I say unto you, <u>That every idle word</u>

that men shall speak, they shall give account thereof in the day of judgment.

37. For by thy words thou shalt be justified, and by thy words thou shalt be condemned.

Then said Jesus to those Jews which believed on him, If ye continue in my word, then are ye my disciples indeed;
John 8:31

Chapter 8
Filled with The Word

Jo. 1:14

And the Word was made flesh, and dwelt among us, (and we beheld his glory, the glory as of the only begotten of the Father,) full of grace and truth.

We've been talking about who Jesus was before He was Jesus. He was the Word of God.

Now, Jesus has arrived on the scene. We could go on and on,...& on, but we need to see this.

The same power God released in Genesis, the same "Word" God released in Genesis, **now lives in you.**

He came along in person in Jo. 14:12-14. & Jo. 15:7. And said some very important things.

Jo. 14:12-14

12. Verily, verily, I say unto you, He that believeth on me, the works that I do shall he do also; and greater works than these shall he do; because I go unto my Father.

*13. And whatsoever ye shall ask in my name, **that will I do**, that the Father may be glorified in the Son.*

*14. If ye shall ask any thing in my name, **I will do it.***

Jo. 15:7

*If ye abide in me, and my words abide in you, ye shall **ask what ye will**, and it shall be **done unto you.***

God has given us what to say, and a way to say it, that will activate, what we said. The promises. Then Jesus comes along and tells us in person that whatever we ask for in His name, He will do that too. That the Father may be glorified in the Son. If we ask anything in His name, He will do it.

Jesus has and always will do what the Father says, but did you notice, He will now do whatsoever we shall ask in His name? Now, old familiar scripture suddenly takes on a new dynamic.

Mt. 17:20

And Jesus said unto them, Because of your unbelief: for verily I say unto you, If ye have faith as a grain of mustard seed, ye shall say unto this mountain, Remove hence to yonder place; and it shall remove; **and nothing shall be impossible unto you.**

Mt. 21:21-22

21. Jesus answered and said unto them, Verily I say unto you, If ye have faith, and doubt not, ye shall not only do this which is done to the fig tree, but also if ye shall say unto this mountain, Be thou removed, and be thou cast into the sea; it shall be done.

22. And all things, whatsoever ye shall ask in prayer, believing, ye shall receive.

Mk. 11:23-24

23. For verily I say unto you, That whosoever shall say unto this mountain, Be thou removed, and be thou cast into the sea; and shall not doubt in his heart, but shall believe that those things which he saith shall come to pass; he shall have whatsoever he saith.

*24. **Therefore** I say unto you,* **What things soever ye desire, when ye pray, believe that ye receive them, and ye shall have them.**

Lk. 17:5-6

5. And the apostles said unto the Lord, Increase our faith.

6. And the Lord said, If ye had faith as a grain of mustard seed, ye might say unto this sycamine tree, Be thou plucked up by the root, and be thou planted in the sea; and it should obey you.

Jo. 16:24

Hitherto have ye asked nothing in my name: ask, **and ye shall receive, that your joy may be full.**

One might say yeah but, Jesus was speaking to His disciples when He said those things. Hey, I've got a word for you, the disciples are no longer here, but I'm here. I'm a disciple. Who are you? Are you a disciple? If you are, He's talking to you.

Heb. 1:1-4

1. God, who at sundry times and in divers manners spake in time past unto the fathers by the prophets,

2. Hath in these last days spoken unto us by his Son, whom he hath appointed heir of all things, by whom also he made the worlds;

*3. Who being the brightness of his glory, and the express image of his person, **and***

**upholding all things by the word of his**
**power,** _when he had by himself purged our_
sins, sat down on the right hand of the Majesty
on high;

4. Being made so much better than the
angels, as he hath by inheritance obtained a
more excellent name than they.

The Bible, is Jesus of Nazareth, in written
form. He is "The Word of God."

From Genesis to Revelation, the Bible is
Jesus in written form. However, in written
form the Bible is like a stick of dynamite. It
has the inherent power in it but it needs to be
ignited. The written Word is inactive, logos.

However, when the Word of God is spoken,
He will manifest Himself by signs following.

_Mt. 18:19-20_
19. Again I say unto you, _That if two of you_
shall agree on earth as touching any thing that
they shall ask, it **_shall be done for them of_**
my Father which is in heaven.
20. For where two or three are gathered
together in my name, **_there am I in the midst_**
of them.

Now here's an interesting scripture. It shows

us that there is power in agreement. Not only that, but when we agree on scripture, that in itself brings Jesus, Himself into our agreement. Now, we are three!! You know Jesus is going to agree with scripture, **He is scripture.** I honestly believe that if we agree, "expecting," Jesus will carry out the agreement with signs following. What do you think? What are you believing for? Are you believing for anything, or just touching all the bases but not actually believing God for anything? Remember, He is in you, He knows what you're thinking, and what you intend, and whether or not you're in Faith.

With the Lord's help I have put together a Bible Study Course called Kingdom Realities. Sixty plus hours of teaching about "The Kingdom of God." we live by our words, not money, not natural ability, power or influence. Remember, it's words only,... in the Kingdom of God, no chainsaws, no cordless drills, no silver, gold, or precious stones by which we can exchange for goods and services. God lives by His Word, and we need to learn to live by our words.

The Bible study can be found in the book, "THE KINGDOM OF GOD, AN AGRARIAN SOCIETY."

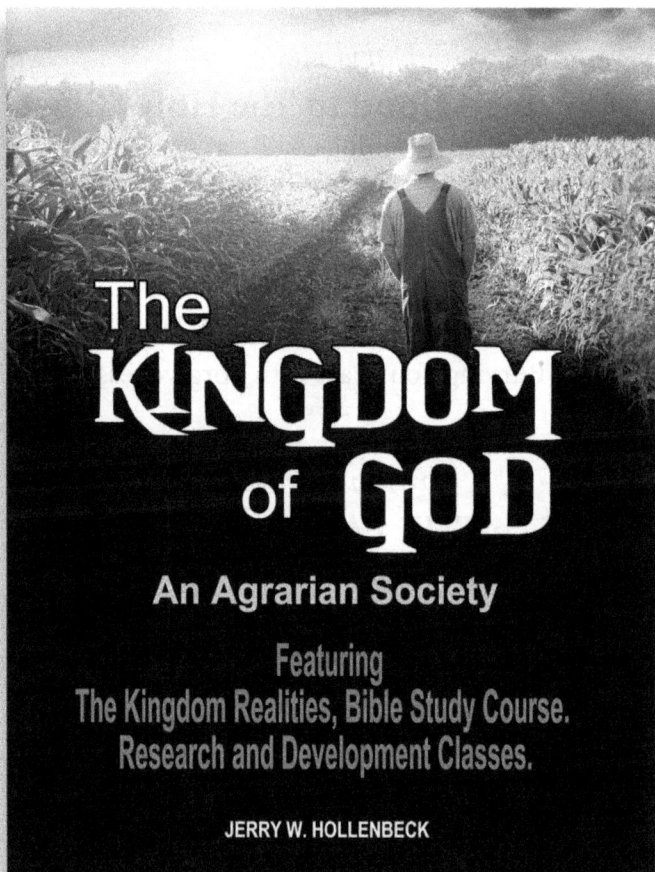